Woman, Why Are You Weeping?

Woman, Why Are You Weeping?

A Lenten Companion for Women

Edited by

Therese Johnson Borchard

A Crossroad Book
The Crossroad Publishing Company
New York

1997
The Crossroad Publishing Company
370 Lexington Avenue, New York, NY 10017

Scripture quotations are from the New Revised Standard
Version Bible, © 1989 by Division of Christian Education
of the National Council of the Churches of Christ
in the United States of America

Acknowledgments will be found on pp. 94-95,
which constitute an extension of the copyright page.

Printed in the United States of America

Library of Congress Catalog Card Number: 97-69606

ISBN 0-8245-1721-0

For all women who are weeping

Contents

Early on the first day of the week, while it was still dark, Mary Magdalene came to the tomb and saw that the stone had been removed from the tomb. . . . Jesus said to her, "Woman, why are you weeping? Whom are you looking for?" Supposing him to be the gardener, she said to him, "Sir, if you have carried him away, tell me where you have laid him, and I will take him away." Jesus said to her, "Mary!" She turned and said to him in Hebrew, "Rabbouni!"

—John 20:1,15-16

Foreword

During Lent, each of us, like Mary Magdalene, stands at the tomb of Jesus . . . waiting . . . and weeping. We confront that which is ugly and dark in us, in hope of beauty and in anticipation of lightness. Each year at this time we die a short death; we let go of that which is finite in order to welcome She who is Infinite. It is the liturgical season of stillness, which inevitably forces us to ask, "What next?"

Women journey together toward Easter. We are with Jesus when he is tempted in the desert; we are with him when he is betrayed by a disciple; and we are there, with his mother, at the foot of the cross when his final hour arrives. We are the women he stops to console; and we are Veronica wiping the sweat from his face with a cloth. On this Lenten road, we experience a common pain, ask similar questions, and sense a universal hope.

In this compilation, readers are invited to make a Lenten journey with some of the great women spiritual writers of our day. Each of the forty days of Lent presents a theme starting with a scripture passage taken from the lectionary readings of the day, following with a selection of text from a popular woman author, and concluding with a prayer.

The daily themes of this book are arranged in a manner that both unites the reader with the rest of the church community in this liturgical season and provides women with a means of journeying together with other women—by way of reflective texts—from weeping (Ash Wednesday) into rising (Easter).

The spiritual writers chosen as part of this collection empower us to search within ourselves for that which is lifeless and dying; their stories and meditations stimulate conversation in ourselves and with others. They help us, at the end of these forty days, to be transformed with Jesus into beauty and light—to find an end to our weeping— so that we may rise with Him on Easter morn.

One Who Weeps for Us,

in the midst of your pain
You flood the earth
with your life's blood,
washing away all that distracts us
from You and one another.
Clarify to us the meaning of our baptism:
that, when the waters recede,
we will be cleansed and empowered
by the tears of your compassion;
Sorrowful Mother,
Divine Child,
Spirit of Mercy.
Amen.

—*Mary Kathleen Speegle Schmitt*

Weeping

> "'Yet even now,' says the Lord, 'return to me with all your heart, with fasting, with weeping, and with mourning.'"
> —*Joel 2:12*

My father had just died before my eyes in the middle of the night. There was within me a child's hope that if I didn't tell anyone or begin to tend to the necessary details, none of it would be true; for a brief moment I wanted to run out into the rain, keeping the night's events in the place of bad dreams. A storm was raging outside, a storm was raging inside, and I was suddenly confronted with a series of questions and decisions that I dealt with in the midst of overwhelming feelings and a desperate need to be quiet.

It seemed unbelievable that the sun could rise after so raw and deep an experience of night. I could not fathom that the cycle of life continued in the day or, bound as I was in a cycle of terror, loss, and grief, that there could ever be a sense of wholeness and resurrection.

The pain was wrenching and made surreal by a lack of sleep and constant stimulation. I felt exhausted and mute. The most desolate moment of the passage was the night after the funeral when the crowds had gone and the emptiness settled upon the house. It was then that I knew the grief would not be neatly handled or wished away from my heart. I had been completely transported in a few moments from the innocence of knowing death as an abstraction to the actual experience of witnessing my father's passage to another world—one minute accessible, the next minute gone, taking with him the luxury of thinking that there would always be more time or another reprieve from death.

—*Teresa Rhodes McGee*

———

Prayer

In weeping be my joy,
My rest in fright,
In sorrowing my serenity,
My wealth in losing all.

Amid storms be my love,
In the wound my delight.
My life in death . . .
—*Teresa of Avila*

Renunciation

"If any want to become my followers, let
them deny themselves and take up their cross
daily and follow me."
—Luke 9:23

B y meditating on Jesus, on the one hand, and
by repeatedly asking ourselves "Who am I,
really?" on the other, we begin to renounce our
sense of our particular personality, that
personality that establishes itself in the world by
its distinction from other personalities. And we
renounce our pride, our sense of valuing ourselves
as someone who is doing something good. We
enter into Jesus' experience of himself as an
instrument of God: God alone is good, and
whatever Jesus does is really the Father's work.
Jesus only does what the Father tells him to do,
or what he sees the Father doing; or else it is the
Father working through him.

And we too are called to become like that.
We are to feel ourselves transparent, so that this
light of the Source can shine through us. It is as
though each of us had been a many-faceted
crystal, painted in various colors. We could see

how we were different and separate from each other because the colored paint made each of us quite visible—by reflected light—as an object with definite boundaries. Now the power of renunciation—letting go our interest in our personality and our pride—dissolves the superficial decorations, washes the painted colors away, and lets the light shine *through* the pure crystal. When this happens, the crystal as such becomes almost invisible, as the light pouring through it floods out to the whole environment.

—*Beatrice Bruteau*

———

Prayer

Lord,
Help me to become
less of myself
and more of You;
to renounce the part of myself
that keeps me from You.
Grant me the strength
to reject all superficiality,
to become transparent,
so that only Your light
may shine through me.
Amen.

Healing

"Your light shall break forth like the dawn,
and your healing shall spring up quickly."
—*Isaiah 58:8*

Healing involves gathering together what has been lost, forgotten, repressed, disowned, and inviting it into one's life again. The Hebrew word that describes this welcoming what has been lost is *tikkun*, which means to heal or to mend what has been broken, to transform it. When we tend our wounds . . . we invite the forgotten or lost part of ourselves back into our life and let go of what does not belong to us.

It is through the process of healing that we become more accepting of ourselves and less fearful of who we are. When we bid farewell to our wounds, we regain the inner energy that has been focused on the hurt. It is often through facing our struggles and painful ordeals that we discover greater clarity and learn what gives our life direction and meaning. We perceive more fully what is truly of value and come to appreciate life at a new depth.

—*Joyce Rupp*

Prayer

Healing God,
come to my hidden corners,
open the doors to my soul rooms
that are tightly locked.

Awaken in me.
Bring to life all my deadness.
Enthuse the depressed emotions.
Reenergize my inner weariness.
Bathe the grime
of my ego-centeredness.
Clarify my confusions.
Fire my neglected loves.
Brush off my dusty dreams.
Nurture my spiritual hungers.
Ease my sore relationships.
Deepen my sense of self-esteem.
Stir up my connection with the world.

Tenderly gather in your arms
all that still needs healing,
all that remains wounded and wanting.
May I grow each day
into greater wholeness
with a stronger, purer inner freedom.
　　　　　—Joyce Rupp

Guidance

"The Lord will guide you continually, and satisfy your needs in parched places, and make your bones strong."
—Isaiah 58:11

We seek out spiritual direction using a variety of words and reasons: healing, training, knowledge, encouragement, a safe place to talk. Fundamentally, however, we seek out someone who knows more than we do. Like a novice seeking a teacher, many of us eventually find that our own resources are not enough and that a guide is needed.

We need someone who has been further along the path than we have been, someone "who knows God better" than we do, because at the deepest level, whether we know it or not, what we really seek is God. We need to know God, to know that we are loved—unconditionally—by God. Once we come to understand that, we can find the things we thought we sought: healing, peacefulness, knowledge of ourselves, connectedness to our world.

That is the work of a spiritual director—
to help us pay attention to and respond to God's
presence in our lives.
—*Debra K. Farrington*

———

Prayer

Guardian of my soul, thank you,
for guiding me in the dark places,
for reaching me through
the people of my life,
for drawing near to love me
when I feel unlovable,
for teaching me how to tend my wounds,
for guarding me with words of truth
and moments of empowerment,
for allowing my pain and struggle
so that I can come to greater wholeness.

Guardian of my soul,
you are my Coach in the Cave,
my Voice in the Fog,
my Midwife of Wisdom.
I place my trust in you
as I give myself to the process
of learning from my darkness.
—*Joyce Rupp*

Day 5
Communion

"Truly I tell you, just as you did it to one of
the least of these who are members of my
family, you did it to me."
—*Matthew 25:40*

The nature of God as inherently *communio*
makes it possible to speak of how the mystery of
God is capable of relating to what is creaturely
and laced with history. Incomprehensible depth
of personal communion, [God] is free to create
the historical universe and relate to it not out of
necessity but out of overflowing graciousness.
. . . Reflecting its Creator, the universe has
relationship as its fundamental code.

The one relational God, precisely in being
utterly transcendent, not limited by any finite
category, is capable of the most radical
immanence, being intimately related to
everything that exists. And the effect of divine
drawing near and passing by is always to
empower creatures toward life and well-being
in the teeth of antagonistic structures of reality.
. . . God's presence among creatures touches them
with power the way fire ignites what it brushes.

We know that fire is present wherever something catches on fire. Everything that exists does so by participation in the fire of divine being.
—*Elizabeth A. Johnson*

———

Prayer

Lord,
Help me to see your face
in everything around me,
To hear your voice
in everyone who speaks to me,
To feel your hands
in all that I touch.

Ignite my heart with the fire
of your divine love,
So that everything and everyone
I meet in my day
Is brushed with the fervor
of its infinite flame.

Amen.

Prayer

"Pray then in this way: Our Father in heaven,
hallowed be your name. Your kingdom
come. Your will be done, on earth as it is in
heaven. Give us this day our daily bread.
And forgive us our debts, as we also have
forgiven our debtors. And do not bring us to
the time of trial, but rescue us from the evil
one."

—Matthew 6:9-13

The most potent and acceptable prayer is the
prayer that leaves the best effects, . . . when the
soul not only desires the honor of God, but really
strives for it, and employs the memory and
understanding in considering how it may please
Him and show its love for Him more and more.

Oh, that is real prayer—which cannot be
said of a handful of consolations that do nothing
but console ourselves. When the soul experiences
these, they leave it weak and fearful and sensitive
to what others think of it. I should never want
any prayer that would not make the virtues grow
within me. If with my prayer there come severe
temptations and aridities and tribulations, and
these leave me humbler, then I should consider
it good prayer, for by the best prayer I mean that

which is most pleasing to God. One must not think that a person who is suffering is not praying. He is offering his sufferings to God, and many a time he is praying much more truly than one who goes away by himself and meditates his head off, and, if he has squeezed out a few tears, thinks that is prayer.

—*Teresa of Avila*

———

Prayer

Lord,
Teach me how to pray
with an open heart,
a willing mind,
a pliable will.

Guide my soul
to that resting place
where I can best hear You,
the silent sanctuary
within myself
where sincerity and humility
alone hear your infinite wisdom.
Amen.

Conversion

"And the people of Nineveh believed God;
they proclaimed a fast, and everyone, great
and small, put on sackcloth."
—Jonah 3:5

On the cover of one of my journals I placed a
print of a woman standing in solitude by a large,
open window. She faces outward, looking into a
mysterious Monet-like woods. There is a
numinous quality to her attentive presence. This
mood speaks to me of the movement between
the conscious and the unconscious, of connecting
the outer world and the inner world. There is a
sense of mystery and wonder. Whatever it is that
the woman is observing, it is obviously reaching
back into the depths of her soul. Something or
Someone beckons to her and holds her there at
the window.

I was attracted to that print because I felt
that I had some of those same soul-searching
moments in my midlife growth. I believe that in
midlife God calls to the soul: "Move beyond what
you know. Now is the time to risk the hidden
path of going deeper. Go into the stillness and
solitude within you. Come, find your true Self."

This is a call to become more grounded or rooted in our strengths and our wisdoms—those inner treasures that wait to be discovered as we enter unknown, inner territory and reflect upon our life.
—*Joyce Rupp*

———

Prayer

Patiently
You wait
for me
to love.

You reach
You whisper
You sing
in silence.

I see
I hear
I know
Your love.

Now
Take me
in quiet
Surrender.

Amen.

Seeking

"Ask, and it will be given you; search, and
you will find; knock, and the door will be
opened for you."
                    —*Matthew 7:7*

We emerge—most of us—from those
transitional, dislocating years of adolescence
aware of a kind of chronic ache that, like a
rheumatism of the soul, will neither leave us nor
entirely disable us. As an ache it hovers between
a low-grade discomfort and a full-fledged
yearning. We wander back and forth between the
two extremes, but we interpret the ache as arising
from a single principle: Once there was a unity
that now is gone. And its corollary: That same
unity is the sacred.

Not God, but that presumed, and
presumably remembered, oneness that in its
living, brilliant particularities is a companionable
whole. That is the sacred. And whether we speak
of individual experience in phrases like "the loss
of innocence" or of speciel experience in stories
like the Garden of Eden one, we mean only to
symbolize our separateness from it while at the
same time asserting our historic right to mourn

for it as something once enjoyed and now lost.

In and from that backward-longing, loss-professing stance, we define our lives through the metaphors of search and quest and journey, and ourselves as travelers upon an often tenuous trail in or up toward the consummation—toward, that is, reconnection.

—*Phyllis A. Tickle*

———

Prayer

I search for God,
elusive, hidden God,
I long to dwell
in the heart of Mystery.

I search for my true self,
more of who I already am,
knowing there's so much
yet to be discovered.

I search for love,
the unconditional love
that enfolds me
and asks to be shared. . . .

I search for Home,
always for Home,
unaware, of course,
that I am already there.

—*Joyce Rupp*

Reconciliation

*"First be reconciled to your brother or sister,
and then come and offer your gift."
—Matthew 5:24*

The quality of our being with one another must be examined carefully before offering our gifts at the altar, for if we recall that anyone has anything against us, then we are to leave our gift at the altar and go immediately to be reconciled. We are to waste no time. Reconciliation takes precedence over worship. In fact, we are incapable of worship, of prayer, of standing in the presence of God or the community if any of us is at odds with another human being. The prelude to all worship and adoration is reconciliation. The word for reconciliation in Greek means "to walk together again," and we are commanded to be at one before we come before God.

Where others stand in relation to us must be of crucial importance, for it reveals more than anything else whether or not we are holy and virtuous according to Jesus' standards of judgment. . . . All holiness begins with life, protection of it, appreciation for it, and nurturing of it. Anger, contempt, abusive language, expressions of violence, deliberate separation from others and our lack of humanness sever the bonds of Jesus' family where all are entitled to forgiveness, mercy, and reconciliation.

—*Megan McKenna*

———

Prayer

The wolf shall live with the lamb,
    the leopard shall lie down with the kid,
the calf and the lion and the fatling together,
    and a little child shall lead them.
The cow and the bear shall graze,
    their young shall lie down together;
    and the lion shall eat straw like the ox.
The nursing child shall play over the hole of
        the asp,
    and the weaned child shall put its hand
        on the adder's den.
They will not hurt or destroy
    on all my holy mountain;
for the earth will be full of the knowledge of
        the Lord
    as the waters cover the sea.

—*Isaiah 11:6-9*

Compassion

"Love your enemies and pray for those who persecute you."
—*Matthew 5:44*

There are to be no limits to love; there is no one we are not required to pray for or intercede for before God. In fact, the new criterion is not our own country or nation or people but our very enemy, both collectively and individually.

If we do obey Jesus' commandment we prove without a doubt that we are children of our Father, for God's sun rises on both the bad and the good. God's rain falls on the just and the unjust. If we love only those who love us, what merit is there in that? The world does as much. In fact, sinners and people we think very little of—tax collectors, politicians, corrupt business corporations, or our enemies—do as much. If we are going to imitate God we are to be perfect as God is perfect! It sounds impossible, outrageous, even naive. In some translations of this famous line the words *compassionate* or *holy* are used instead of the word *perfect*.

Loving one's enemies is as natural as God loving us, but it is only with awareness of God's tenderness that this phenomenon becomes utterly apparent. This experience of God, as Simone Weil says, "is not consolation, it is light." Perhaps it is both realities: light that makes us see others with God's gentle eyes, and consolation that the only way we can respond to that love in our own experience of God is to look with such eyes upon all human beings, especially our enemies.

—*Megan McKenna*

———

Prayer

Lord,
Help me to see others
with the same compassionate eyes
with which You look
upon Your people.

Enable me to listen to others
with the same loving ears
with which You hear
Your children's cries.

Teach me to love others
perfectly, unconditionally,
as You do.
Amen.

Caregiving

"Give, and it will be given to you . . ."
—*Luke 6:38*

A spirituality of care is a tough, earthly spirituality. In the concreteness of giving and receiving care we live out the gospel injunction to love both ourselves and others well. We experience and mediate Christ's love.

Many women spend a lifetime in caregiving: raising children, supporting aging parents, being there for friends in need. They do not want to stop caring; it is a satisfying source of meaning and identity. . . .To feel no longer of use is one of the sorrows of age, as conveyed by the Jewish tale: "A young woman once said to an old woman, 'what is life's heaviest burden?' And the old woman said, 'to have nothing to carry.'"

It is not hard to see that caregiving requires a deep and constant caring for self. But we find ourselves in conflict as we weigh competing demands. We try to spread our limited resources among endless claims and desires, knowing that there is simply not enough to cover them all. Women bear the costs of care personally in terms of lost sleep and health, stressed relationships, compromised personal goals. When resentment starts to rise, we fear it is because we do not know how to love, that we are no longer generous enough to care for others. Resentment is rather the signal that things are out of balance. . . . We cannot postpone the care of self until all other claims are met; it must happen all along the way.

—Kathleen Fischer

———

Prayer

Word-made-flesh:
God understands a woman's world
and the work of her hands:
the stress of feeding a multitude
with too many mouths and too little food;
a wedding feast and no more wine:
"Woman, is that a concern of mine?"
"Well, yes," she said,
and the vintage flowed;
and sometime later,
when a cup was passed at a Supper
that would be the last,
a promise was made
so that there would always be enough for all.
—Miriam Therese Winter

Day 12

Listening

"Hear the word of the Lord . . . Listen to the
teaching of our God."
—*Isaiah 1:10*

Our whole life ought to become an exercise in
listening attentively—to the words of Holy
Scripture, to the writings of spiritual masters, to
the wise counsels of good people, invested with
authority.

Despite our zeal for the Lord, we must
be patient. . . . As a musician seasons his or her
style, years may go by before we develop an ear
to appraise rightly every epiphany of the Mystery.
We may even mistake God's voice for our own,
but at least we are trying to listen.

To a hearing heart, a message once
garbled becomes clear; a path thought to be lost
is found. At times, though rarely, genuine
locutions may accompany faith-filled listening.
The back-and-forth discourse between us and the
Divine is like the ebb and flow of the sea. We do
not wait for thunderous disclosures. We listen to
the still, small voice at the core of our being and
try our best to respond. Once we allow the Spirit

to take the lead, useless worry recedes. We learn
the wisdom of surrender.

—*Susan Muto*

———

Prayer

Lord,

Teach me how to listen.
Still the inner stirring
of my heart,
Pacify my anxious thoughts,
Quiet the noise
that distracts my soul,

So that I may hear—
really hear—
What You
and others
Are saying to me.

Amen.

Day 13
Self-Offering

"Whoever wishes to be first among you must be your slave."

—Matthew 20:27

Christ's death was the new Passover, the revelation of the meaning of the era to come. Human beings could no longer project their "sacrifice" onto the animal creation and confine their efforts to the control of instincts through law. This had been a necessity for the growth of consciousness; but the sacrifice of the Lamb of God became a symbol of the conscious offering possible for individual human beings—the offering of one's whole self, instinctive, affective, reasoning, even the divine nucleus of one's being.

Eventually men and women could learn to offer themselves and to become "brothers of Christ" by living their own hypotheses to the bitter end. "I live, yet not I, but Christ liveth in me," said St. Paul. The ego-centered personality had to be transformed and to become conscious of the life of the Self—a sacrifice which could only be accomplished through the power of love.

—Helen M. Luke

Prayer

Thus says God:
I will be heard!
Make flesh
of my every word:
give peace, justice, liberty
visible reality;
feed the hungry,
don't just meet
and plan
what they will one day eat.
Shelter the homeless,
help the poor,
the destitute,
the insecure.
Preach with your hands,
wear out your shoes:
words alone are not Good News.
   —*Miriam Therese Winter*

Trust

"Blessed are those who trust in the Lord,
whose trust is the Lord."
—Jeremiah 17:7

Not long ago, during Sunday morning worship, I saw a young black man holding his infant daughter in his arms. The little one seemed fascinated with her father's voice. She had placed her face square in front of his and was watching his lips. The young man was swinging rhythmically with the music, almost dancing with his child. Gurgling with delight, she placed her little fingers on his lips and finally put almost her entire hand into his mouth, totally secure in his love. The image of this child's joy and safety in her father's presence was a powerful prayer experience for me.

I wonder if what prevents so many of us from letting ourselves be free, or at least, what seems to make it so difficult for us to accept the resurrection process, is not a deep-down insecurity, a fear and mistrust of God's blessings. Our contemporary Christian dislike and misunderstanding of pain seems matched only

by our suspicion of happiness even, paradoxically,
as we crave it.
                            —Barbara Fiand

———

Prayer

Holy Trinity,
Mystery of loving communion,
Invitation to deeper union.
Grant me the grace to pass
The test of trust.
Teach me to be self-donating,
To express freely
A commitment to mutuality,
To ever loving,
Quietly befriending reciprocity.
Strengthen my will to love
My sisters and brothers
As you love us and all others.
                            —Susan Muto

Day 15

Anger

"But when his brothers saw that their father loved him [Joseph] more than all his brothers, they hated him, and could not speak peaceably to him."
—Genesis 37:4

Women in American society are conditioned to deny their pain, and to smooth over or ignore the effects of violence, even when it is directed against them. As one sister said to me, "Women seem to have trouble drawing the line between what is passive acceptance of suffering and what can transform it." This is the danger that lies in Emily Dickinson's insight that "Pain—is missed—in Praise": that we will try to jump too quickly from one to the other, omitting the necessary but treacherous journey in between, sentimentalizing both pain and praise in the process.

The sister, speaking of the women she counsels—displaced homemakers, abused wives, women returning to college after years away— says, "It doesn't help that the church has such a lousy track record here. We've said all these crappy things to people, especially to women:

'Offer it up,' or 'Suffering will make you strong.'
Jesus doesn't say these things. He says, 'This will
cost you.'"

—*Kathleen Norris*

———

Prayer

Why, O Lord, do you stand far off?
　　Why do you hide yourself in times
　　of trouble?
In arrogance the wicked persecute the
　　poor—
　　let them be caught in the schemes
　　they have devised.

For the wicked boast of the desires of
　　their heart,
　　those greedy for gain curse and
　　renounce the Lord.

Rise up, O Lord; O God, lift up your
　　hand;
　　do not forget the oppressed.

Break the arm of the wicked and
　　evildoers;
　　seek out their wickedness until you
　　find none.
　　—Psalm 10:1-3,12,15

Celebration

"We had to celebrate and rejoice, because
this brother of yours was dead and has come
to life; he was lost and has been found."
—*Luke 15:32*

To sacramentalize is to pay attention. It is what
a community does when it names and claims
ordinary human experiences as holy, connecting
them with history and propelling them into the
future. There are no magic tricks nor impossible
dreams. It is simply taking time to attend to the
people around us, to see in real lives (not in novels
nor in Scripture) the stuff of human existence:
birth, pain, growth, bonding, breakup, loss,
friendship, and to recognize it as such. This is
what sacraments are for. They are concrete
experiences with food and touch, dance and
drink, prayer and silence, affirmation and music.
Think of a good dinner party. What could be
holier?

People recognize something about their
experience when a similar one is brought to
attention. For example, I recently attended a
festive dinner party in celebration of the tenth

anniversary of the couple who were hostessing. In a brief comment between courses they explained the significance of the day for them and thanked their friends for being a part of their life together. It was sacramental.

Celebration is needed not only in the moments of change or loss but in the normal course of relationships to mark their stages and to encourage their deepening.

—Mary E. Hunt

———

Prayer

Loving Creator,

Thank you
for celebration and ritual,
and sacraments.
For the gathering together
of family and friends,
and those I love,
For personal stories shared
over bread and wine,
And for occasions filled with
dance and music,
and laughter.
Amen.

Restoration

"Go, wash in the Jordan seven times, and your flesh shall be restored and you shall be clean."
          —*2 Kings 5:10*

Restoration is generally a long work. Absolution is the business of a moment, but the reconstruction and healing of a damaged personality, the calling back of the divine likeness into a distorted human heart, proceeds neither quickly nor smoothly.

Gardens take time, effort, cultivation. They are a symbol of this drawing forth of material and spiritual creation from our personal chaos, a symbol of this moral and human restoration.

That is the way conversion works. We cannot give over our own hearts to the pruning, planting, and cultivating action of God without taking with us the rest of the world. In the deepest part of ourselves, we share its soil, its rain and sun; and the only way we can isolate ourselves from the rest of the world is by refusing to surrender our own hearts to this work. For the process of seed, growth, and harvest go on within the paschal offering of Christ. He is our ground and our fruition.

—*Miriam Pollard*

———

Prayer

Woman of Transforming Power,
in the midst of the wasteland
You create an oasis
where trees shelter us
from the blazing sun.
Invite us to drink
of your living waters:
that, leaving behind the places
of death,
we enter into the community
whose promise is Shalom.

—*Mary Kathleen Speegle Schmitt*

Forgiveness

> "'Lord, if another member of the church sins against me, how often should I forgive? As many as seven times?' Jesus said to him, 'Not seven times, but seventy-seven times."
> —*Matthew 18:21*

To "for-give" is to give abundantly; the prefix in the verb is an intensive. And so our attitude to any and all, enemies and adversaries included, should be a clear will that the person have life and have it abundantly.

Thus forgiveness means entering into the lives of other persons in order that they may be and that they may be abundantly. We unite with them in their present living moment, loving them as they are. If multitudes of persons were to become free in this way, we all would begin to experience a sense of the Whole as an organic reality, as a single Living One, as a Divine Body. We would be the real *Corpus Christi*.
—*Beatrice Bruteau*

I remember once using the familiar . . . image of the sea . . . to explain the relationship between love and forgiveness. The sea would be

God's love; forgiveness was what happens when we turn and walk into it, or stop shivering on the pebbled shore or running around in the skirts of an incoming tide. The sea is always there, always itself; forgiveness is not a decision on God's part to be nice to somebody awful who has come to the point of reformation. Forgiveness is what happens when we walk right in and give ourselves to the waves and the gulls and the deep green mystery of the floorless ocean. It is love seen from the point of view of someone who has been afraid or unwilling to approach its wild, salt bounty.

—*Miriam Pollard*

———

Prayer

We ask forgiveness
for assuming we know
all there is to know
about each other,
for presuming to speak
for each other,
for defining, confining,
claiming, naming,
limiting, labeling,
conditioning, interpreting,
and consequently oppressing
each other.

—*Miriam Therese Winter*

Discipline

"But take care and watch yourselves closely, so as neither to forget the things that your eyes have seen nor to let them slip from your mind."
—*Deuteronomy 4:9*

I learned that when you go to church several times a day, every day, there is no way you can "do it right." You are not always going to sit up straight, let alone think holy thoughts. You're not going to wear your best clothes but whatever isn't in the dirty clothes basket. You come to the Bible's great "book of praises" through all the moods and conditions of life, and while you may feel like hell, you sing anyway. To your surprise, you find that the psalms do not deny your true feelings but allow you to reflect on them, right in front of God and everyone.

I soon realized, during my first residency at St. John's, that this is not easy to do on a daily basis. Before, I'd always been a guest in a monastery for a week or less, and the experience was often a high. But now I was in it for a nine-month haul, and it was a struggle for me to go to choir when I didn't feel like it, especially if I was depressed (which, of course, is when I most needed to be there). I took great solace in knowing that everyone there had been through this struggle, and that some of them were struggling now with the absurdity, the monotony of repeating the psalms day after day.

I found that, even though it took a while—some prayer services I practically slept through, others I seemed to be observing from the planet Mars—the poetry of the psalms would break through and touch me. . . . For all of their discipline, the Benedictines allowed me to relax and sing again in church; they allowed me, as one older sister. . . described it, to "let the words of the psalms wash over me, and experience the joy of just being with words."

—*Kathleen Norris*

———

Prayer

Creator,
Help me to harness
my fleeting passions and
my wavering desires;
Help me to channel my creativity,
and direct my energy to You.
Teach me the art of consistency
and the beauty of discipline.
Amen.

Solidarity

"Every kingdom divided against itself
becomes a desert, and house falls on house."
—*Luke 11:17*

Women of Ethiopia, my sisters, I am haunted
by my memories of you, for you are to me every
woman, and your deprivation is every woman's
pain. When I had to turn you away with no kilo
of grain and no cup of oil because I had none to
give, I felt the emptiness and the hunger of all
women everywhere who hover on the edge of
survival, who lack life's basic necessities, who
are deprived of opportunity, of fundamental
human rights. . . . When I sat in your woman
circle, shoulder to shoulder, while the monsoon
rain ran rivers of mud along the walls of our
grass-roof hut, I was pierced to the heart with
your wail of agony as you closed your baby's
eyes in death, and I heard our Mother God howl
in pain at your pain, felt Her cradle your child,
Her child, close to Her maternal heart.

Women of the world—of the First World,
Fourth World, of the North and of the South,
women of poverty and of privilege, of every

culture and every color, of every country and every clan—we are, all of us, sisters. We stand together in the face of injustice. We stand together in solidarity. We stand for integrity for all people. We will make every effort to overcome whatever would divide us, the exclusion perpetuated by religious and social systems, the hierarchy of position and the priority of gender, the oppressive distinctions of caste or class.

—*Miriam Therese Winter*

———

Prayer

Before we can pray,
before we can dream,
before we can witness
to justice and peace,
we must be a single circle,
a single, unbroken circle,
a wide open,
welcoming circle.
Let us build this circle of love.

—*Miriam Therese Winter*

Friendship

"You shall love your neighbor as yourself."
—Mark 12:31

The creative love of Mother Wisdom reaches throughout the universe and all of its embedded individual lives with a friendship brimming with desire for the well-being of the whole of her creation. Human beings experience that the vivifying, liberating, and creating power of the holy mystery of God engages us in partnership to renew the earth and establish justice in such a way as to turn us also in an attitude of profound friendship toward all others, even those most unlike ourselves.

Holy Wisdom, the horizon encircling all horizons, is a profound mystery of relatedness, whose essential livingness consists in the mutuality of friendship. The love of friendship is the very essence of God.
—Elizabeth A. Johnson

Prayer

We give thanks
that we are all part
of the family circle of God,
forgiving one another,
loving one another
because God has first loved us,
that God's Spirit
has banished distinctions
between Jew and Greek,
between slave and free,
between female and male,
between those who are in power
and those who are powerless.

We give thanks
that we are one
in the love of the One
who loves in us,
forever and ever.
Amen.
    —*Miriam Therese Winter*

Day 22

Humility

"For all who exalt themselves will be
humbled, but all who humble themselves
will be exalted."
—Luke 18:14

Through self-love, we make ourselves the center
of the universe. Self-will makes us want our own
way. Self-interest leads us to make decisions and
manipulate people and situations to our own
advantage, no matter how badly they affect
others. When we are self-conscious, we are so
full of self, we cannot allow anyone else a
significant place in our vision of reality. We are
our own worst enemies. If we cannot eradicate
selfism, we become insufferable egotists,
wreaking havoc within ourselves and in the world
around us—in our marriages, families, and our
short-sighted business practices around the globe.

The vanity of self-esteem makes us look
in the wrong places for personal worth—outside
instead of inside, at material goods instead of
inner value. We get caught up in the world's
mendacity, the Big Lie, and falsely esteem

money, possessions, social or economic status, rank, seniority, the prestige of some office.

The vanity of self-esteem and preoccupation with human approval lead us to become soft and self-indulgent instead of challenging ourselves and stretching our limits. We seek rest instead of struggle, false security instead of holy insecurity, vapid peace instead of spiritual warfare. We become bourgeois, lax, lukewarm, and merely "ok" and "pretty good." . . . The surest antidotes to this mediocrity are searching self-knowledge, vigilance, and humility.

—*Tessa Bielecki*

———

Prayer

Loving Maker,
Remind me always that
I am merely dust,
and to dust I shall return;
that everything I am
and all that I accomplish
is You in me.
Direct all of my efforts
and daily work
toward the honor and glory
of Your heavenly kingdom.
Amen.

Creativity

"Be glad and rejoice forever in what I am creating."

—*Isaiah 65:17*

Clarissa Pinkola Estes in *Women Who Run with the Wolves* defines creativity as "having so much love for something that all that can be done with the overflow is to create." If we do not create, we perish. Or as Estes says, if a woman surrenders the passion of accomplishment, she loses her basic joy. The process of creation brings joy: "her life's blood, spirit-food and soul-life all in one."

Take your creative pulse. As when we take a pulse on wrist or throat, we may grope for it at first. But when we find it, we know the spot. We feel the surge of blood beneath the skin; we recognize the unique, personal rhythm. We nestle into our niche, our unique form of creativity with the satisfaction of a teenager ploughing into pizza or a nursing baby snuggling into the breast.

A runner in the movie *Chariots of Fire* says, "when I run I feel God's pleasure in me." Adapt that statement to fit yourself.
    —*Kathy Coffey*

———

Prayer

A small, wooden flute,
an empty, hollow reed,
rests in her silent hand.

it awaits the breath
of one who creates song
through its open form.

my often-empty life
rests in the hand of God;
like the hollowed flute,
it yearns for the melody
which only Breath can give.

the small, wooden flute and I,
we need the one who breathes,
we await one who makes melody.

and the one whose touch creates,
awaits our empty, ordinary forms,
so that the song-starved world
may be fed with golden melodies.
    —*Joyce Rupp*

Day 24

Fertility

"Wherever the river goes, every living
creature that swarms will live."
—*Ezekiel 47:9*

I enjoy working in a garden even though it can
be hard work. I don't mind digging out weeds
and I like to gather vegetables and fruit, but I
detest readying the soil for planting. After a long,
hard winter the ground can be packed solid from
heavy snows or pelting, drenching rains. The soil
can be difficult to turn over. It resists the hoe or
the garden tiller and it may take many hours of
tiring work before the earth is soft and porous.

   This part of gardening is essential,
however, if green shoots are to push their way
through the soil. A garden that has a hard, packed
surface will not be able to receive the life-giving
moisture of the spring rains. The water will run
off and fail to soak the soil. Earth that is turned
over is essential for a garden's watering.

   The human spirit is much like a spring
garden. If growth is to happen, it too must be
made ready. The human spirit must be opened
up if God's goodness is to grow there. Open
minds and hearts are ready to receive the

abundant life God constantly offers. This kind of
opening up is at the heart of the Easter story.

—Joyce Rupp

———

Prayer

Flowing River,
water of fluidity and power,
You carve the imprint
of your Being
into the earth-banks past
which you surge.

Sculpt our lives
and the life of your church
by the movement of your Spirit:
that we draw from the brief span
of our mortality
the good that you long for us
to know;
through the begotten, crucified,
and risen One.
Amen.

—Mary Kathleen Speegle Schmitt

Suffering

"For the Lord has comforted his people, and
will have compassion on his suffering ones."
—*Isaiah 49:13*

Women who have suffered need to find a
different way of naming God out of the darkness.
Can such women identify with the crucified man
Jesus? Can the image of the suffering male bring
healing to women who have been wounded by
men? The cross with the crucified Jesus is
Christianity's most powerful icon of God
suffering with humanity, but I wonder whether
we do not also need female icons of suffering
and compassionate love. . . . Perhaps we do not
need so much to depict the body of a woman on
the cross as to recognize that every raped and
beaten female body is the body of Christ. God
suffers in the bodies of women: "A voice in
Ramah is heard . . . Rachel is weeping for her
children" (Jeremiah 31:15).

The woman who cannot forget her
sucking child, who will ever have compassion
on the child of her womb, images God for us.
Rachel becomes an icon of God's compassion—

suffering with her children. Rachel and her children of the Holocaust, of war, of famine, of slavery, of rape and abuse, of torture, name God. Paradoxically it is those who have known the absence of God—Rachel, Hagar, Job, and all who cry out with the crucified One 'Why didst thou bring me forth from the womb?', 'My God, my God, why have you abandoned me?'—who can testify to the presence of God, who can speak of God, who can image God.

—*Anne Thurston*

———

Prayer

Lord,
Be with me in the hour
that I, like you, cry aloud,
Why hast thou forsaken me?
Help me to find peace
in moments of aloneness,
understanding
at times of confusion,
and serenity
always.
Amen.

Rejection

"I have come in my Father's name, and you
do not accept me."
—John 5:43

In his death the Christian story of shame
mysteriously comes full circle: Jesus is naked and
unashamed. But now the exposure is not the
romantic nakedness of the primeval garden, but
the degrading exposure of a public execution. Yet
the humiliating circumstances of this death did
not humiliate Jesus: he disregarded the
shamefulness of the cross. Embracing his death,
Jesus transforms the power of social shame.
Christians celebrate this transformation in their
devotion to the crucifix; what at first seems to be
a shameful failure, to be concealed in
embarrassment, is raised up as a sign of suffering
that has been healed.

The way that Jesus dies, the manner and
dignity with which he embraces his end, saps
death of its absurdity and its sting. The pain of
death is not magically removed, but its
degradation and humiliation are lifted. Because
he has died this way, every other death becomes
more tolerable, less absurd. But the mysterious

transformation his death provides extends beyond physical death to every traumatic experience of shame. Christians who have suffered severe abuse in childhood bring their shame to prayer and religious liturgy. There they encounter someone who has survived profound social shame—Jesus who has been humbled without being destroyed. Though ridiculed, his worth has not been squandered. Though exposed in all his vulnerability, he has not been found inferior. Rejected by society, he has been embraced by God. This extraordinary event encourages Christians to dare expose their hidden shame to the Lord and feel its power dissolve.

—*Evelyn and James Whitehead*

———

Prayer

Blessed are you
when people revile you
and persecute you
and utter all kinds of evil
against you falsely
on my account.
Rejoice and be glad,
for your reward is great in heaven,
for in the same way they persecuted
the prophets who were before you.
—*Matthew 5:11*

Trial

"Let us test him with insult and torture . . .
and make trial of his forbearance."
—*Wisdom 2:19*

B efore wholeness is possible, descent is necessary. In the myth of Inanna, she must descend through the seven gates, leaving part of her clothing behind until at the end she enters naked into the presence of her shadow Self, Ereshkigal. In Christian myth Jesus moves from Galilee, where he is applauded, to Jerusalem, where he is crucified. Each of us at some time in our lives . . . moves through a kind of descent to discover who we truly are and where it is we are called to go in our life's journey.

It is our capacity for evil that assaults us and overwhelms us. We have the choice, as in Gethsemane, for succumbing to our capacity for evil, or for grasping the darkness within us as the chaos of creative energy for good. We welcome desire but turn from greed. We welcome anger but turn from destruction. We welcome sorrow but turn from self-pity. We submit all that would turn us from our true Self . . . to the nails of consciousness that tame the undisciplined energy that has pushed us hither and yon in the wilderness journey. Only having suffered the nails of crucifixion do we come to the brink of the wholeness promised in Easter.

—*Mary Kathleen Speegle Schmitt*

———

Prayer

Lord,
Be with me
in the desert
where I am offered
an entire kingdom
for the price of my integrity.

Stay at my side
in the Garden of Gethsemane,
when I, like you,
ask the Father
to let my cup pass.

Disclose to me
the ugliness evil hides.
And guard me always
from the lure of temptation.

Amen.

Wisdom

"It was the Lord who made it known to me,
and I knew."
—*Jeremiah 11:18*

We think of wisdom as a gift of age. What is this elusive and mysterious quality? Observation tells us that it does not happen automatically; we can surely grow old without becoming wise. One element of wisdom is the accumulation of experience and the good judgment that results. But we hope for more—that as we age we will come closer to the very meaning of life. We have followed many routes to happiness, feasted at countless tables in an effort to still our hungers, placed numerous objects at the center of our lives. Yet something is still missing. "Mid-life for women," a friend told me, "is a matter of the heart. We find the gifts of the Spirit within: wisdom, compassion, perception." As women of wisdom, we return at last to the truth of our being, the ultimate mystery of the universe, the sacred dimension of existence.

In the Bible the figure of Sophia, or Wisdom, is a female personification of the gracious presence of God in the world, inviting human beings to relationship. . . . She offers wisdom as God's gift, bringing true knowledge, prudence, and discernment. She promises that when we attend to the divine message, we will find joy and delight.

—*Kathleen Fischer*

———

Prayer

Happy are those who find wisdom,
    and those who get understanding,
for her income is better than silver,
    and her revenue better than gold.

She is more precious than jewels,
    and nothing you desire can compare
      with her.
Long life is in her right hand;
    in her left hand are riches and honor.

Her ways are ways of pleasantness,
    and all her paths are peace.
—*Proverbs 3:13-17*

Light

> "I am the light of the world. Whoever
> follows me will never walk in darkness but
> will have the light of life."
> —*John 8:12*

Easter is a word most of us have used all of our
lives, yet I suspect few of us have thought about
its derivation. . . . The root of the German word
for Easter, *Ostern*, is the ancient Aryan word for
both east and dawn. It is thought that *Ostern*
became *Easter* because the name of the dawn-
goddess was Eostre. . . . [Christianity] was an
alien religion for the Germanic peoples, so for
them the greatest feast of the new faith became
easily associated with their own great goddess
who nurtured the light of the sun as he rose from
the darkness of the night.

It seems to me that in our time, this image
of the goddess bringing to birth the resurrected
sun—or Son—out of the womb of darkness, out
of the burial cave in the earth, carries a numinous
power.

—*Helen M. Luke*

Prayer

God of passionate life,
who sends the sparks,
who lights the inner blaze
and tends the flame,

Fill us with your radiance.
Enkindle us with your love.
Touch us with your goodness
so that we will be the kindling
of your generous compassion.

—*Joyce Rupp*

Despair

"The people spoke against God and against
Moses, 'Why have you brought us up out of
Egypt to die in the wilderness?'"
                    —*Numbers 21:5*

Hope and despair are not opposites. They are
cut from the very same cloth, made from the very
same material, shaped from the very same
circumstances. Most of all, every life finds itself
forced to choose one from the other, one day at a
time, once circumstance after another. The only
difference between the two is that despair shapes
an attitude of mind; hope creates a quality of soul.
Despair colors the way we look at things, makes
us suspicious of the future, makes us negative
about the present. Hope, on the other hand, takes
life on its own terms, knows that whatever
happens God lives in it, and expects that,
whatever its twists and turns, it will ultimately
yield its good to those who live it well.

When tragedy strikes, when trouble
comes, when life disappoints us, we stand at the
crossroads between hope and despair, torn and
hurting. Despair cements us in the present; hope
sends us dancing around dark corners trusting in

a tomorrow we cannot see. Despair says that there is no place to go but here. Hope says that God is waiting for us someplace else. Begin again.
—*Joan Chittister*

———

Prayer

Lord,

Walk with me
from my darkness
to the light of Easter.

Meet me at my tomb of despair
with your healing power.

Help me to choose hope
time after time
so that I can always
begin again.
Amen.

Day 31

Truth

"You will know the truth, and the truth will
make you free."
—John 8:32

It is precisely in the meaninglessness, in the
experience of no-thing of everything that is, of
everything that has been achieved, that finally
the flute is readied for music; and slowly, so very
painfully, we begin to realize that having
achieved all the hopes and dreams of our youth,
having gained, in other words, "the entire world,"
[we] will ultimately remain worthless and
insignificant without the transcendence that calls
us into the surrender of our ego-power and the
giving up of our control over particular events,
goals, achievements, and even relationships into
the stillness that underlies them all and holds
them together in meaning.

Slowly, very slowly, this transcendence
leads us through pain, through prayer, through
friends—companions on the journey, through
dreams, through reflection, and ultimately
through surrender not only to know ourselves
more deeply, but also to love ourselves. It does

this primarily because of the insight that comes through suffering: One learns to let-be, to hold oneself in one's poverty. One learns that poverty is blessed; that the hungry will be filled; that one is loved because one *is*, not because one *does*. One learns about the brotherhood and sisterhood of the human family; about the responsibility that truly loving another calls forth, the freedom and empowerment it entails. One learns of the commonality of sin and of redemption that was always there, waiting, and never needed to be earned or "lived up to." One heals even as one recognizes the "sting in the flesh," and in the healing one becomes whole.

—Barbara Fiand

———

Prayer

Lord,
Help me to shed the layers of ego
I have grown in fear
of disclosing my true self,
in thinking that I am loved
for what I do,
not because I simply am.
Help me to be,
just be,
the person You formed.
Amen.

Commitment

"I will establish my covenant between me
and you, and your offspring after you
throughout their generations."
—*Genesis 17:7*

H ow is life to be lived well? Most of us are
intrigued by the question. We recognize that our
lives are likely to hold some dark times, periods
of confusion or loss or pain. But we search for
ways of living that, over a lifetime, will be both
satisfying and effective. Satisfying: so that our
life makes sense to us personally, bringing us joy
and meaning and peace. And effective, so that
our life makes sense beyond just ourselves. We
want to make a contribution, to help other people,
to give ourself to the larger world. To live this
way means to link ourself to people and to values.
We do this by developing a capacity for
commitment.

Philosopher Hannah Arendt captures the
importance of this capacity when she says, "The
remedy for unpredictability, for the chaotic
uncertainty of the future, is contained in the
faculty to make and keep promises."
Commitments rescue life from being a series of

random encounters interrupting our isolation. We link our lives to people and to values in the hope that we may learn to be fruitful in consistent ways.

Personal commitment is the core strength in intimacy. In our commitments we pledge ourselves *for the future*—beyond both our vision and our control. This risk is necessary, for without commitment we limit our loyalties to the present. But this risk is also serious because we do not control the future. We cannot be certain that our present feelings will last. In a commitment, we summon our will in an effort to shape the future. We hold ourselves open to whatever is necessary so that the bond between us may endure.

—Evelyn and James Whitehead

———

Prayer

Lord,
Grow my capacity for commitment,
which transforms a series
of random events
into a lifetime of meaning,
and imitates your profound loyalty to us.
Empower me to say yes
to what I cannot see and do not know
and to surrender my control
to the cause of faithfulness.
Amen.

Solitude

"Jesus went away across the Jordan . . . and
he remained there."
——*John 10:40*

The dynamics of solitude and a community of
shared interest are, I believe, essentials of the
creative life. Solitude, as poet May Sarton notes,
"cracks open the inner world." Creative leaders,
thinkers, artists—these seem especially marked
and strengthened by solitude. Catherine of Siena
in her room voluntarily cut off from the social
intercourse of her home, John of the Cross in the
Tower, Florence Nightingale on her sickbed,
Malcolm X in solitary confinement, Van Gogh
in Arles, Nelson Mandela in a South African
prison, and of course, Jesus in the desert—for
all these and so many more, unseen solitude
offered a spaciousness where the secrets of the
soul could be explored and given form.
——*Dolores R. Leckey*

We speak a great deal in America today
. . . about centering. As a presently in vogue,
subjective buzzword, *centering* is good for
talking about just about everything from

meditating on the mind of the Buddha to slipping back for a little rest into the forest clearing. That is, it gives a name to the intentional gathering of the attention into one focus that in its quietness, like a glass lens held to the sun, will burn a hole in the obstructing membrane between now and no time—a recognition . . . that the sacred is somehow within us.

—Phyllis A. Tickle

—

Prayer

Lord,
Provide for me
a room of my own,
a secret garden
or hidden place,
where I am free
to create
and pray
and be.
Amen.

Faith

"Many of the Jews therefore, who had come
with Mary and had seen what Jesus did,
believed in him."
—John 11:45

One of my favorite Bible stories is the healing
of the epileptic boy in Mark 9. It is a story of the
helplessness and powerlessness experienced by
Jesus' disciples, who when approached by the
father of the sick boy are unable to cast the demon
out. They stand paralyzed before the suffering
of the possessed son and his grieving father and
consequently are subjected to the scorn and
ridicule of a group of scribes and Pharisees in
public. When Jesus comes on the scene, instead
of consoling his friends, he makes clear to them
that their inability to heal the boy signifies their
lack of faith. He pronounces them a "faithless
generation." If they believed in the power of life,
they would participate in that power and thus be
able to do what they think only Jesus can do:
perform a miracle.

And when the boy's father fervently
beseeches Jesus to heal his son but qualifies his
appeal with "if you can do anything," Jesus

rebukes him as well: "If you can! All things are possible to him who believes" (Mark 9:23). In other words, when will you finally abandon this if-you-can talk? When will you finally give up your impotence, your weakness, your unbelief in the healing power of God?

I learned from this story that one of God's names is "All is possible," and I know that if I cannot talk to All-is-possible, if I do not listen to All-is-possible, if I do not believe in All-is-possible, then I am dead. Thus my prayer would be to ask All-is-possible to be present.
—*Dorothee Söelle*

———

Prayer

Almighty God,
All-is-possible,
Help me to believe
without signs,
to know
without miracles.

Strengthen my faith
so that I can
surrender all doubt
and unbelief.
Amen.

Day 35

Beauty

"Mary took a pound of costly perfume . . .
anointed Jesus' feet, and wiped them with
her hair. The house was filled with the
fragrance of the perfume."
—*John 12:3*

If life is anything at all, it is, for most of us most of the time, dullness punctuated by the unpredictable. For the most part, we get up day after day, month after month, year after year to do the same things over and over again. Take out the garbage. Do the wash. Attend the meeting. Fill out the forms. Get the job done. Go shopping. Make the telephone calls. Do the dishes. Visit the relatives. Meet the deadlines. Over and over and over again we grind our way through one year after another: holding the fort; running the line; keeping the faith. Dull. Boring. Beautiful.

One of life's best—and slowest—lessons is that it is in ordinariness where God waits for us. It is in the ordinary that we too often miss the Sacred Presence. So inured are we to life around us that we don't even see it anymore. While we touch the holy in our very hands we look for it elsewhere.

Don't take beauty for granted. It is sometimes found in the ugliest places, sometimes lost in the richest, sometimes forgotten in the dullest, always abandoned when what is most effective is preferred to what is most soulful.

—*Joan Chittister*

———

Prayer

Lord,
Heal my blindness—
my failure to see
the beauty
that surrounds me.

Restore my vision—
that cannot appreciate
the kindness
of your creation.

Awaken my heart—
to Your presence
in the mundane,
in the ordinary,
in the moments
of my every day.
Amen.

Birth

"The Lord called me before I was born;
while I was in my mother's womb he named
me."

—Isaiah 49:1

The God who created the earth, the sea and the sky, the God who created the mountains and valleys is found here in the most intimate and hidden place—within the womb. The creative activity of God takes place in the weaving and 'knitting together' in the womb. This is the God who gives birth to creation, who gives birth to us. Birthing mothers image the birthing God. We are not all mothers but we are all born from the womb of mothers. We have all shared the experience of birth, we will all know death. We are connected by our beginning and by our end.

Giving birth provides us with a unique insight into creative, creating pain, into life coming out of death, into the boundaries which must be negotiated when we move into new life. Birthing mothers image the creative activity of God and provide us with an appropriate metaphor for the Divine.

—Anne Thurston

Prayer

She knows my fragile hand,
the curve of my fingerprint.
She knows how each hair waves
when the wind buffets my brow.

She knows my singing heart,
the center of myself—
Where She forms
her dwelling place.

In my mother's womb,
She shaped her home—
In me,
before the rim of time.

She is my forever Mother—
Fixing me with her eye
in the smiling palm
of her opened hand.

Motherhood

"The Lord God has given me the tongue of
a teacher, that I may know how to sustain
the weary with a word."
—*Isaiah 50:4*

We may deliver a baby, but we never separate
completely from that life that has been so much
a part of ours. Just as the bloodstream and food
supplies once intermingled, now we connect in
less tangible ways. We may no longer worry
about alcohol or nicotine crossing the placenta,
but kids' stresses still show up in our bodies: *our*
stomachache during *their* driving test, *our* pain
during *their* penicillin shot, *our* headache as *their*
fever mounts.

It must be some bizarre compensation for
those of us who never figured out the papoose
wrap. We may have flunked Swaddling 101, but
we spend the rest of our days inextricably tangled.
Maybe it's the memory of that baby powder
fragrance, the utter dependence of that tiny
creature that keeps us forever bound. Maybe it's
the experience of leading intertwined lives.
Whatever the cause, it enlarges our hearts past
the bursting point, makes us bigger than we ever

thought we could become. Whatever the reason, the old song was right: "Blessed be the ties that bind."

—Kathy Coffey

———

Prayer

Mother of All Creation,
in the universe, your Womb,
we are sustained as of one body
with You.
Protect us by your fierce love,
and assure us that we are safe
with You:
that we radiate the strength and warmth
of your nearness to all the world.
—Mary Kathleen Speegle Schmitt

Intimacy

> "Jesus knew that his hour had come to depart from this world and go to the Father. Having loved his own who were in the world, he loved them to the end."
>
> —*John 13:1*

How do we live in ordinary intimacy with the people, events, and things that enter our world both expectantly and unexpectantly?

Let me clarify something from the start. Whether you are male or female, young or old, single or married, believer or nonbeliever, neither you nor any human being on the face of the Earth can survive as distinctively human without receiving and giving the gift of ordinary intimacy. This common way of contact connects us with one another in tears and laughter, in sorrow and joy.

The faces of intimacy are as diverse as stars, as unique as snowflakes. Pick up any book of portraits, any record of history, and you will see what I mean. Walk through any park on a summer's day and catch a couple in love smiling into each others' eyes. Stop by a hospital room and observe the way a compassionate nurse bathes the fevered brow of a sick child. See how a mechanic touches with pride the car he has repaired, and you'll see another sign of recovered intimacy. It happens to us when we really trust another person, when we receive selfless love, and when we take care of things like good stewards do.

—*Susan Muto*

———

Prayer

Lord of love and light
From whom flows
every blessing bright,
Teach me to imitate your caring,
Sharing generosity.
Draw me into splendid
Moments of recovered intimacy
Full of compassion
and tender mercy.
Teach me to be trusting
Of my own and others' vulnerability.
Make me a recipient
Of your graces,
Bestowed abundantly.

—*Susan Muto*

Death

"When Jesus had received the wine, he said,
'It is finished.' Then he bowed his head and
gave up his spirit."
                              —John 19:30

In Holy Week, "leaf by leaf by leaf," we examine and embrace our deep woundedness. We struggle in the throes of the death of our old self. We resist. We do not want to let go of what we are or who we have been. We want to enter into New Being, but as who we are. We do not want to change, not even the worst of our bad habits or distorted attitudes. The more we resist, the more we choke out our life, and the farther we find ourselves from new life.

As Mother Pelican [a medieval tradition depicts Christ as a mother pelican who was understood to pierce her own breast so that her children could survive by feeding from her blood], the Divine chooses to die in and with us, to nurture us even in the midst of death.

—Mary Kathleen Speegle Schmitt

Prayer

Mother Pelican,
You pierce your own heart
so that your children may live.
Fill us with your steadfast love:
that, dying with You,
we also rise with You
to dwell forever
in the Land that flows
with milk and honey.

Bird of Paradise,
Crucified One,
You are the Spirit
who flies to the ends of the earth.
Amen.
—*Mary Kathleen Speegle Schmitt*

Rising

"Do not be afraid; I know that you are
looking for Jesus who was crucified. He is
not here; for he has been raised, as he said."
—*Matthew 28:5-6*

Several weeks ago my son Patrick said to me,
"I'll bet if you had a magic lamp you would wish
you weren't sick." Cherishing his tender hopes
for my health, I asked myself if I would wish
away the illness. And my truthful first impulse is
that I would wish it away with death-defying
speed. But since I have no magic lamp, and since
defying death is no longer part of my illusion, I
have to make a different choice. That choice is
to let myself be remade in the experience of
illness and believe in the sanctity of the journey
of life itself. I celebrate that sanctity in an
embodied truth that leads me to buy spinach and
quilt life's mysteries in front of an empty tomb.

When all is said and done, I offer thanks
that in the midst of pain I have been given the
great gift of life, not as I planned it to be, but
better, infinitely better, because my limitations
are stitching my life to the backing of the living
God. I, who wanted to conquer and change the

world, instead find myself connected in pain and powerlessness to sources of life much deeper than my own ego and much more enduring than my own ability to order reality. Such is the grace in my stiffness and pain, a simple joy in being alive, a music that leads me home. And such is the powerful blessing of the God who truly, and simply, is love.

—*Teresa Rhodes McGee*

———

Prayer

Risen Lord,

I saw you fall on the road to Calvary,
and heard the pounding of nails
into your flesh.
I was there as you consoled your mother,
and when you bowed your head to death.

Now I stand
outside your empty tomb,
and ask the guards where they
have taken you.

"He has risen,"
they say to me,
"as he said he would."

Acknowledgments

We wish to acknowledge the following publishers for permission to reprint previously published material.

From *Autumn Gospel* by Kathleen Fischer. Copyright © 1995 by Kathleen Fischer. Used by permission of Paulist Press.

From *Because of Her Testimony: The Word in Female Experience* by Anne Thurston. Copyright © 1995 by Anne Thurston. Reprinted by permission of The Crossroad Publishing Company.

From *The Cloister Walk*. Reprinted by permission of Riverhead Books, a division of The Putnam Publishing Group from THE CLOISTER WALK by Kathleen Norris. Copyright © 1996 by Kathleen Norris.

From *The Comforter: Stories of Loss and Rebirth* by Teresa Rhodes McGee. Copyright © 1997 by Teresa Rhodes McGee. Reprinted by permission of The Crossroad Publishing Company.

From *Dear Heart, Come Home: The Path of Midlife Spirituality* by Joyce Rupp. Copyright © 1996 by Joyce Rupp. Reprinted by permission of The Crossroad Publishing Company.

From *Embraced by Compassion: On Human Longing and Divine Response* by Barbara Fiand. Copyright © 1993 by Barbara Fiand. Reprinted by permission of The Crossroad Publishing Company.

From *Experiencing God with Your Children* by Kathy Coffey. Copyright © 1997 by Kathy Coffey. Reprinted by permission of The Crossroad Publishing Company.

From *Fierce Tenderness: A Feminist Theology of Friendship* by Mary E. Hunt. Copyright © 1991 by Mary E. Hunt. Reprinted by permission of The Crossroad Publishing Company.

From *Hidden Women of the Gospels* by Kathy Coffey. Copyright © 1996 by Kathy Coffey. Reprinted by permission of The Crossroad Publishing Company.

From *Lent: The Daily Readings* by Megan McKenna. Copyright © 1997 by Megan McKenna. Reprinted by permission of Orbis Books.

From *Late Have I Loved Thee: The Recovery of Intimacy* by Susan Muto. Copyright © 1995 by Susan Muto. Reprinted by permission of The Crossroad Publishing Company.

Excerpted from *May I Have This Dance?* by Joyce Rupp. Copyright © 1992 by Ave Maria Press, Notre Dame, IN 46556. Used with permission of the publisher.